DUDLEY SCHOOLS
LIBRARY SERVICE

KU-719-721

Schools Library and Information Service

S00000632932

Radical Sports

CANOEING

Phil Revell • • • • • • • • • • •

www.heinemann.co.uk
Visit our website to find out more information about **Heinemann Library** books.

To order:
 Phone 44 (0) 1865 888066
 Send a fax to 44 (0) 1865 314091
Visit the Heinemann Bookshop at www.heinemann.co.uk to browse our catalogue and order online.

First published in Great Britain by Heinemann Library, Halley Court, Jordan Hill, Oxford OX2 8EJ, a division of Reed Educational and Professional Publishing Ltd.

Heinemann is a registered trademark of Reed Educational & Professional Publishing Limited.

OXFORD   MELBOURNE   AUCKLAND
JOHANNESBURG   BLANTYRE   GABORONE
IBADAN   PORTSMOUTH NH (USA)   CHICAGO

© Reed Educational and Professional Publishing Ltd 2000

The moral right of the proprietor has been asserted.

All rights reserved. No part of this publication may be reproduced, stored in a retrieval system, or transmitted in any form or by any means, electronic, mechanical, photocopying, recording, or otherwise without either the prior written permission of the Publishers or a licence permitting restricted copying in the United Kingdom issued by the Copyright Licensing Agency Ltd, 90 Tottenham Court Road, London W1P OLP.

Designed by Celia Floyd
Originated by HBM Print Ltd, Singapore
Printed in Hong Kong by Wing King Tong

ISBN 0 431 03674 8 (hardback)
04 03 02 01 00
10 9 8 7 6 5 4 3 2 1

ISBN 0 431 03683 7 (paperback)
04 03 02 01 00
10 9 8 7 6 5 4 3 2 1

British Library Cataloguing in Publication Data

Revell, Phil
    Canoeing. – (Radical sports)
    1. Canoes and canoeing – Juvenile literature
    1. Title
    796.1'22

Acknowledgements

The Publishers would like to thank the following for permission to reproduce photographs:

Action-Plus, p. 14 (Steve Bardens), p. 26 (Richard Francis); B & C Alexander, p. 4; Weymouth Canoe Lifeguard Association/Don Berry, pp. 20, 22, 23; Mountain Camera/John Cleare, pp. 18-19; Perception Kayaks, p. 7; Robert Harrison, p. 29; Tony Tickle, pp. 5, 6, 8-9, 10-13, 15-17, 21, 24, 27, 28.

Cover photograph reproduced with permission of Frank Spooner/Gamma

Our thanks to Mike Devlin at the British Canoe Union for his comments in the preparation of this book.

Every effort has been made to contact copyright holders of any material reproduced in this book. Any omissions will be rectified in subsequent printings if notice is given to the Publisher.

Any words appearing in the text in bold, **like this**, are explained in the Glossary.

This book aims to cover all the essential techniques of this radical sport but it is important when learning a new sport to get expert tuition and to follow any manufacturers' instructions.

DUDLEY PUBLIC

L   45785

632932   SCH
J797.122

CONTENTS

Ancient history

Thousands of years ago someone somewhere sat on a floating log or tree trunk and, using their hands as paddles, drifted **downstream**. Perhaps a piece of wood was used as a paddle. A solid log is heavy, so to lose some of the weight the log may have been hollowed out. And the **canoe** was invented.

Further developments

In different parts of the world primitive humans used whatever materials were available to build better boats. Native Americans made river canoes using the bark from birch trees wrapped onto a timber frame. The Inuit people made seal-skin **kayaks**, and sewed themselves into the **cockpit** to prevent freezing water swamping the tiny boat.

Today, most canoes are made from fibreglass or plastic. Kevlar, a type of very strong lightweight fibreglass, is often used for competition designs. Plastic boats are made using **polyethylene**, a tough material that can be moulded to shape.

An Inuit hunter in his kayak.

Canoes and kayaks

There are two main types of canoe. The open canoe, first used by Native Americans, is a sturdy craft that can carry two or three people and their possessions. The canoeist uses a single-bladed paddle and kneels on the floor of the boat. The canoe has no top surface or **deck**.

CANOE FACTS

> Pacific Islanders used **outrigger** canoes to travel vast distances – over 4800 km in some cases.

The kayak was developed from the Inuit craft and is usually for one person. The kayaker sits in the boat and uses a double-bladed paddle. A **spraydeck** covers the cockpit to prevent water splashing into the boat – but today's **paddlers** don't sew themselves in!

This book is going to look at the single person, decked canoe – the kayak.

River running – an exciting and dangerous sport.

Touring kayak

Many experienced **paddlers** own several **kayaks**. A good kayak to start off with is the plastic touring kayak. It should have a large **cockpit** to make getting in and out easier. Canoe stores should be willing to let you try out a kayak before buying it. Clubs will often lend a boat to new members until they have bought their own.

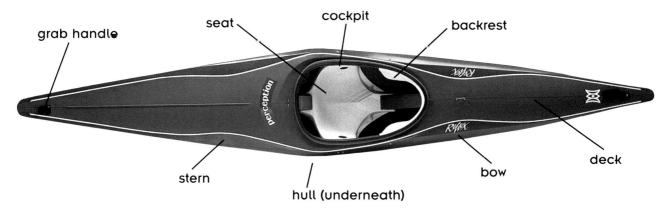

seat — cockpit — backrest

grab handle

stern

hull (underneath)

bow

deck

Essential parts

Every kayak should have something to keep it from sinking. This can be a block of plastic foam secured to the inside, or buoyancy bags filled with air and kept behind the seat. Kayaks must be fitted with a footrest, and a **grab handle** or toggle at both ends of the boat. It helps if there is a backrest fitted and some boats have an adjustable seat which makes it easier to achieve a snug fit.

The power that a paddler uses to propel the boat needs to be anchored. Experienced paddlers will have a close footrest, backrest and thigh grips – all these make sure that the power of the paddle stroke goes where it should – into the water.

Kayaks can be carried by the grab handles.

CANOE FACT

- A canoe's speed is dependent on its size. Longer boats are faster, shorter ones are slower.

TOP TIP

- Never try to lift a boat that is full of water. It will be much too heavy. Turn it on its side to drain the water out.

Types of boats

Boats come in all shapes and sizes. They range from touring kayaks which are suitable for beginners to high specification expedition boats for **white water** paddling on the world's roughest rivers. There are **slalom** kayaks, as on page 6, which are designed for fast turns and weigh less than a couple of kilograms. Modern kayaks need very little maintenance and plastic boats are strong and difficult to damage.

A **playboat** for hot-dogging and **rodeo** paddling. This is short and stubby to allow for fast turns and acrobatic manoeuvres.

A sea kayak stands out with its long sleek lines.

This is a recreational kayak which is suitable for beginners.

WHAT ELSE DO YOU NEED?

Warmth and safety

Even on a hot summer's day rivers and lakes may be cold, so **paddlers** need to ensure that they are well-prepared for the difference between air and water temperature. A hundred years ago a male paddler wore a straw boater, tweed jacket and trousers. Things have changed a bit for today's kayakers who have a whole wardrobe of specialist kit to keep them safe and warm.

Helmet

Helmets are a must in shallow waters and in fast-flowing rivers or the sea. Check that your helmet fits well and has a firm chinstrap. A helmet should fit snugly so that there is no movement when you shake your head. But it should not be too tight over your forehead. Always fasten the strap.

Cagoule

A water-proof cagoule (cag) is an essential piece of equipment. It has elasticated cuffs and neck to keep the water out and enough room to allow you to move freely.

Buoyancy aid

A **buoyancy aid** is essential. You should never go canoeing without one. You wear a buoyancy aid like a waistcoat. It's not a lifejacket – it is filled with foam not air. It should fit snugly with a cord or strap around your waist.

Wetsuit

A wetsuit is advisable, even in summer, although as a beginner you can sometimes get by with an old tracksuit and pullover. A full body wetsuit is called a **steamer**. A kayaker's wetsuit, with no arms, is a **long john**.

Footwear

Sports sandals or wetsuit boots are best for your feet. Thick-soled trainers or shoes with long laces that could get tangled on the footrest should be avoided.

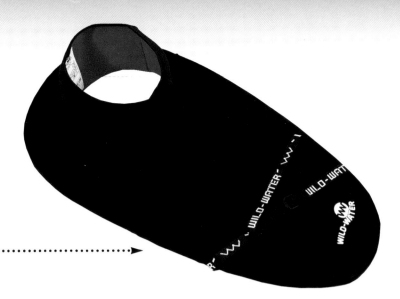

Spraydeck

The spraydeck is worn around your waist like a skirt and fits over the rim of the **cockpit** to keep water out. As a beginner you can start off without one, but a spraydeck makes canoeing much more comfortable.

Paddles

Paddles can be made from wood, metal or plastic and are usually **feathered**. This means that the blades are at different angles. This allows for a more natural wrist and shoulder movement. There are different paddles for different types of canoeing. Test for the right paddle size for you by stretching your fingers over the top blade, most paddles are between 190 and 210 cm.

SAFETY TIP

In the sea, even in summer, a swimmer's survival time without a wetsuit and buoyancy aid is less than three hours. The body loses heat very quickly when immersed in cold water.

FIT FOR PADDLING?

Canoeists use their whole body when they make a paddle stroke. Their arms and shoulders make the stroke, their trunk twists. Legs grip the sides of the boat and feet push against the footrest. Flexibility is often more important than strength.

Exercises

To prepare yourself for paddling make sure you start with a warm-up by stretching your muscles. This will prepare them for the work they are about to do. Jog or skip on the spot for 10 minutes. Then try each of these exercises, repeating each five times.

Shoulder stretch

Start by making large circular movements with your arms. Keep your fingers pointed and stretch out as far as you can.

Leg stretch

Stand up with your feet shoulder-width apart and slowly reach down to the ground in front of you. Stay standing and cross one leg in front of the other and walk your fingers down the leg as far as you can. You may have to stop at the knees, or you may be able to 'walk' off your toes and onto the ground. Just go as far as you feel comfortable.

Back stretch

Sit in the boat holding the paddle in front of you. Lean back and try to make the paddle **loom** touch the rear **deck** of the boat. Now lean forwards and touch the front deck.

Back and stomach stretch

While still in the boat reach forwards and try to make the left-hand paddle blade touch the right-hand side of the boat as far forward as you can. ·················▶

SAFETY FIRST

 Exercises should be done slowly to avoid pulling or tearing muscles.

Diet

Kayaking is a high energy sport that requires a good level of fitness. This means that you have to eat properly and have a balanced diet.

Too much sweet and fatty food is not a good basis for training. So if you want to be an up and coming kayaker you should avoid chocolates and fried foods. You should eat healthy proteins such as fish and cheese, along with fruit, vegetables and healthy carbohydrates such as bread and baked potatoes. Bananas offer a good mix of carbohydrates, natural sugars and vitamins. The body digests bananas slowly, so they are an ideal snack on a training day.

Getting Started

At the swimming pool

The best place to learn kayaking is in a swimming pool. There is no special equipment needed in the pool, just swimwear. The water is warm, clear and clean and if you're nervous you can have an instructor standing by you.

Many pools have a set of **kayaks** and in the winter months most clubs run pool sessions for beginners and experienced **paddlers**. It's a good place to meet other paddlers from the local canoe club. Good clubs can offer instruction and links to national organizations such as the British Canoe Union and a ready-made group of people to go canoeing with.

In a pool you can make a start on the basic strokes. You could also try these without a paddle, using your hands.

Canoe Polo

🌊 Canoe polo takes place in swimming pools. It's like water polo, but with boats. Competitors wear helmets with face guards to protect them from the swinging paddles.

Safety First

🌊 Boats are heavy and have no brakes. Swimmers should not play in the water alongside **canoes** or kayaks, either in a pool or in the sea.

.... *How to get into your boat*

When you take your kayak out the first thing you need to learn is how to get into it! First, sit on the river bank next to the boat, slide one leg into the **cockpit**, then move over until you're sitting on the rear **deck**. Slowly slide down onto the seat.

Paddling forwards

To move forwards look at the front deck and imagine you can see your feet. Hold the paddle blade away from your chest – imagine that it's covered in foul smelling goo and hold it away from your nose. Place the paddle blade in the water alongside your toes. You will need to stretch forward, twisting the body. Pull the water past you. Now try it on the other side.

Changing direction

To turn, place the paddle alongside your toes and keep your arm straight. Work the blade away from the boat through a complete arc, so it ends up behind you. The trunk of your body will twist and your foot nearest the paddle blade should be pressed hard on the footrest.

How to get out

To get out, place your hands on the deck behind you and ease your weight onto the rear deck. Then slide one leg out onto the bank, followed by your body. If your paddle is strong enough, use it to keep the boat stable by resting it across the rear deck and the bank.

PLACID WATER

Peaceful places

Placid means peaceful, and placid-water canoeing takes place on canals, lakes and slow-moving rivers. Most beginners start on placid water as it's a good place for building up basic skills. In deep water, helmets are not necessary and many **paddlers** also dispense with the **spraydeck**.

Most beginners start on placid water.

Keeping in a straight line

A ship moves forward because it has its engines pushing it through the water using screws at the rear. A rudder keeps a ship going in a straight line. In a **kayak** the 'engine', or source of power, is you in the middle and there is no rudder. For most beginners the result is a boat that refuses to go in a straight line! It takes time to learn the strokes, but after a couple of sessions, most people start to pick up the basics and begin to get their boat under control.

This low brace is keeping the paddler upright even though his whole weight is on the blade.

SAFETY FIRST

Never **canoe** or kayak alone. Experienced paddlers have a simple rule: 'Less than three there should never be.'

Keeping in balance

You can get a surprising amount of support from a paddle blade. A **brace** is when the blade is laid flat on the water. It's a **support stroke** which works in a similar way to when a mountain biker puts their foot down to the ground – it stabilizes the canoe as it turns.

Moving Water

Be prepared!

Moving water can mean a fast-flowing river or the sea. In both settings the water can sneak up on an unwary **paddler**, so before canoeing in moving water make sure that you are well-prepared. To survive the worst of **white water** conditions, paddlers have to learn a new set of skills. The effort is worthwhile so that you can enjoy the buzz of overcoming the elements and pitting your skills against the power of a raging river.

When entering the flow of water raise the upstream edge of the boat with your knee and **brace** the boat with your paddle by holding it flat on the water. This is called a **break in**.

Canoe Facts

- In an **eddy** the water appears to move uphill. In fact, it's recirculating back into the main flow. The boundary between the eddy and the flow, the eddy line, is an area of disturbed water as the fast-flowing river reacts against the quieter water of the eddy. Beware of mini-whirlpools and upflows, which paddlers call **boils**, in these areas.

A **break out** is when you leave the river flow and enter the quieter water nearer the bank – the eddy. But you still need to lean into the turn, like a biker leaning into a bend.

Special skills

If water flows onto the flat upper surface of your boat, its weight will unbalance the **kayak** and cause a **capsize**. So you must 'edge' **downstream**, tilting the boat slightly to keep the **upstream** edge above the waterline.

Experienced paddlers will inspect a rapid to find out what hazards may lie ahead. If a section looks too dangerous they will **portage**, or carry their boats around. If they run the rapid they might have **bank support** which means that someone stands by with rescue equipment.

SAFETY FIRST

Even a slow-moving river is dangerous. You should never paddle on moving water without experienced leaders alongside to advise and assist.

RiVeR RUNNiNG

River running can be an easy-going day trip down a slow meandering river, or a heart stopping, adrenaline filled expedition requiring a support crew and exceptional kayaking skills. Either way the kayaker will need to know what hazards to look out for.

Stoppers

When water drops over a ledge it forms a **stopper**, so-called because a boat running into one will stop dead in the water. Water is forced to the bottom of the river and flows **downstream** along the river bed. On the surface, water flows into the stopper – this **upstream** flow can trap kayakers and is one of the most dangerous features on any river.

Strainers

A tree in the river will have water flowing through its branches. Anything that floats into the branches will be held in place by the force of the water. Even on slow-moving rivers, trees are a hazard to be avoided.

Rocks and obstructions

Underwater rocks can **capsize** a boat and surface rocks can **pin** a **paddler** in the same way as a tree.

A stopper with surface water flowing upstream into the **hole**.

CANOE FACTS

🛶 In 1976 the river that flows down from Mount Everest, the Dudh Khosi in Nepal, was paddled from a height of 5334 metres by a British team led by Dr Mike Jones. Sadly, Dr Jones was killed trying to rescue another paddler on a later expedition.

RIVER GRADING

🍂 Rivers are graded from 1–6:

Grade 1	Not difficult, an obvious route with no obstructions.
Grade 2	Moderate. Some rapids and obstructions, but the way down is still obvious.
Grade 3	Difficult. Larger waves and rapids, obstructions and falls. Route still recognizable.
Grade 4	Very difficult. Similar to grade 3 but the difficulties are more serious and the route is less obvious.
Grade 5	Extremely difficult. Will require a bank inspection and exceptional paddling skills.
Grade 6	Cannot be paddled without serious risk to life. Multiple obstructions and hazards, complicated route or no clear route.

🍂 Most rivers have different grades for different sections. For example, the Zambesi in Zimbabwe is graded from 4 to 6.

This exploration boat enters a part of the Trisuli River in Nepal known as Double Rock Rapid.

SAFETY FIRST

🍂 Don't rely on the river grade. A grade 1 river can become dangerous in flood conditions. Getting information about the river from local sources is important.

ROCK AND ROLL

One of the most impressive tricks a kayaker can perform is the **Eskimo roll**. Experts can roll so fast that bystanders don't realize that they have **capsized** at all. There are even hand rolls in which the kayaker does not use a paddle.

In freezing waters

Rolling is a form of self rescue and to the Inuit it certainly wasn't a party trick. If an Inuit capsized, every second was vital. He had to escape the freezing water temperatures before it was too late. His hunting partner would put his boat alongside and the capsized Inuit would pull himself upright using the bow of his friend's boat.

An Eskimo rescue – the capsized kayaker uses his friend's boat to pull himself upright.

Capsize drill

The best place to learn to roll is in a swimming pool where the water is clear. A diving mask will help you see what is happening underwater. Before practising the Eskimo roll make sure you have mastered the capsize drill in which you get out of the boat while capsized. This is an essential skill. It will mean that you can leave the boat under control and without panicking. The trick is to wait until the boat is completely upside down, then push the boat away as if it were a pair of trousers.

Hip flick

If you capsize you have to use your legs and hips to swivel your boat back upright – an important part of the manoeuvre is the hip flick. Once you have mastered this skill you can go on to learn the Eskimo roll. In this manoeuvre the capsized **paddler** uses an underwater sweep to pull his or her body to the surface and the hip flick to bring the boat upright.

1 Set up with the paddle alongside the boat.

2 Sweep out and over the head.

3 As the boat rotates flick the hips to keep the movement going.

SAFETY FIRST

Never practise rolling alone and always make sure that the **grab handle** on your **spraydeck** is easily available.

RESCUE

It may never happen but ...

Kayaking is a safe activity, although things can go wrong. Possible problems include a hidden rock or tree branch, a wobbly beginner or a misjudgement. When incidents happen kayakers have to be ready for them.

On some beaches and at canoeing events you may see canoe lifeguards who have been trained to use their canoeing skills to rescue people. The lifeguards on this lake are forming a raft to rescue a paddler in the water.

Throwline

Experienced **paddlers** will carry a full rescue kit, but anyone kayaking on a river should at least have a **throwline** and know how to use it.

Practise throwing a line – it's not as easy as it looks. If you're the person in the water requiring help, you must hold the rope to your chest and float on your back. The rescuer should 'play' you like a fish, pulling you into the bank slowly. If there is too much tension on the rope you will find it hard to hold on.

In an x-rescue the rescuer empties the victim's boat.

X-rescue

In deep water at sea or on a lake, where there is no nearby bank, the **x-rescue** can be important. It involves getting the victim back into his or her boat. As the rescuer you pull the victim's flooded boat across your **deck**, tilting it to empty out the water. This is harder than it sounds because a flooded boat is heavy. The victim waits in the water with the paddles, holding on to the **grab handle** at the front of the boat. Once the victim's boat is empty he or she can get back into the kayak while you hold it steady.

SAFETY FIRST

- Never ever, tie yourself, or anyone else, to a rope while canoeing, even in a rescue. The risk of getting tangled up is much too great.

RESCUE KIT

- Throwline: 10 metres of strong rope that floats on water.

- **Loops** and **karabiners**: with these a canoeist can set up a pulley to extract a trapped boat.

- Survival bag: to keep the casualty warm until help arrives.

- First aid kit: check that the container is waterproof.

Sea **kayaks** are much closer to the original Inuit craft than plastic river boats. Sea **paddlers** have rounded Cape Horn, circumnavigated the British Isles, crossed the Tasmanian Sea and traversed the Great Lakes. The boats are long, sleek and fast, with **deck** hatches for storing food and equipment.

Sea kayaks are silent and can go close inshore where other boats would run aground. As a result sea paddlers can get close up to wildlife like seals and birds.

Avoiding difficulties

Sea paddlers have to be able to navigate and understand the weather. A wrong decision could lead to disaster. In difficult sea conditions, the paddler must use the paddle as a rudder. This **stern rudder** keeps the sea boat from broadsiding or **broaching**.

Surf's up

Surf kayakers use special kayaks or **surf skis** in the same way that surfers use their boards and ride the energy of the waves onto the beach. A surf kayak can travel at speeds of 30 kph or more.

The trick is to wait for a wave to form and then paddle hard inshore, matching its speed. The wave will pick up your kayak and then you must use your paddle as a stern rudder to keep the boat on line, **peeling off** the wave it breaks.

CANOE FACTS

- The water in a surf wave is going nowhere. It appears to rush towards the beach, but only at the very edge is there any movement. Waves are a result of the wind pushing against the water and creating an up and down movement, called a swell. The waves crashing onto Bondi beach in Australia were born far out in the ocean, sometimes thousands of kilometres away.

SAFETY FIRST

- Don't try paddle surfing if you're a beginner because it requires a lot of skill. An out-of-control kayaker can be a danger not only to the kayaker, but to other people in the water. Sea paddlers also need to be aware of tides and currents. Never take a boat onto the sea without finding out about these. Contact the coastguard for information.

Paddle surfing can be a lot of fun but make sure you know about the sea conditions first.

COMPETITIONS

There are any number of competitive canoeing events ranging from Olympic **slalom** to marathon racing. The Devises to Westminster marathon race in Britain attracts school teams, kayaking clubs and Armed Services teams over a canal and river course that can take three days to complete.

Slalom

Slalom is an Olympic event, and competitions take place on river rapids. The **paddlers** have to try to run the course as fast as they can. Gates are pairs of light poles hanging over the water. A course can have up to 25 gates and paddlers have to go **downstream** through green gates and **upstream** through red ones. Slalom boats are usually made from fibreglass, for lightness and strength. They are designed for speed and manoeuvrability.

Anyone can compete in slalom – events range from beginners' events, which any paddler can enter, right up to international competitions.

Paddlers must try to go through the slalom gate without touching the poles.

Sprint

This involves **kayak** racing over placid water and is the other Olympic canoeing event. Distances raced are from 200 metres to 10,000 metres and boats can have a crew of four.

White-water racing

This involves kayakers paddling down a grade 3 or 4 river as fast as they can. The course is usually about 30 minutes long and the racing boats' wing design helps with both speed and stability.

Rodeo

Since the development of short plastic **playboats** a new canoe sport has taken off. It's called **rodeo**, and the idea is to perform all kinds of acrobatics with the boat. Paddlers use the power of a river wave or **hole** to stand the boat on end, throw it in the air or spin round in a cartwheel. Points are awarded for each move. It's amazing what some paddlers can make their boats do!

A member of the Japanese team performing a **pop out** at a rodeo competition in Australia.

STARS OF THE SPORT

Olympics

French slalomist Myriam Jerusalmi took the bronze medal in the 1996 Atlanta Olympics. Gold went to Czech Stepanka Hilgertova, with German Oliver Fix taking the men's gold.

1998 Slalom World Cup

World champion Paul Ratcliffe (UK) scraped ahead of American Scott Shipley in the 1998 **Slalom** World Cup, where Stepanka Hilgertova took the Women's No. 1 position.

Paul Ratcliffe – World No. 1.

Shaun Baker

Briton Shaun Baker, dominates the new and dangerous sport of **extreme kayaking**. He holds three world records for kayaking down huge waterfalls, including the vertical drop world record of an unbelievable 19.7 metres. Shaun began kayaking at the age of ten, and six years later led his first expedition – over 1000 kilometres around the coastline of England, Scotland and Wales.

CANOE FACTS

Dana Chaldek of the USA won the silver medal in the 1996 Atlanta Olympics.

In the Second World War the Royal Marines used canvas **kayaks** to carry out a raid on the port of Bordeaux in occupied France. The kayaks were folded so that they could be passed through the hatch of a submarine. The raid was led by Major 'Blondie' Hasler.

GLOSSARY

bank support paddlers who stand by with rescue gear while another paddler 'runs' the rapid

boil swirl of water caused by the friction between the river flow and an eddy, can be very violent

brace a support stroke

break in entering the flow on a river

break out leaving the flow or entering an eddy

broach when a canoe is forced sideways onto a wave (quite often leads to a capsize)

buoyancy aid a jacket padded with foam used to keep a swimmer afloat

canoe a small boat paddled by someone facing in the direction of travel

capsize when a boat tips up and turns upside down

cockpit where the paddler sits in a kayak

deck the upper surface of a boat

downstream (or downriver) the direction the water is flowing

eddy a quiet stretch of water near a river bank or downstream of an obstruction such as a rock

Eskimo roll a self-rescue manoeuvre

extreme kayaking the high-risk sport of paddling where most people would think it was impossible. For example, down waterfalls, on underground rivers and in very remote areas

feathered paddle blades that are not parallel to each other

grab handle a loop or toggle at the front and back of a canoe

hole dangerous re-circulating river wave, also called a stopper

karabiner ovals of strong metal with an opening gate. They can be clipped onto fences, ropes, boats or buoyancy aids.

kayak a decked canoe based on the Inuit design

long john a lightweight wetsuit with no arms, worn by kayakers

loom the part of the paddle between the blades that you hold on to

loop metre-wide circles of a very strong material which can be used with karabiners and a fixed anchor point to set up a pulley

neoprene elastic material that acts as an insulator even when wet

outrigger a pole or hull attached to a boat to provide additional stability

paddler a kayaker or canoeist

peeling off a surfing term meaning to turn sideways and back out to sea, to avoid being swept onto the shore by the breaking wave

pin to be trapped against an obstruction such as a rock or a tree by the force of the water

playboat a short plastic boat designed for unusual manoeuvres

polyethylene strong durable plastic that can be moulded into different shapes

pop out rodeo manoeuvre in which the paddler forces the boat to exit vertically from the water

portage from the French 'to carry'. It means to walk around a rapid or obstruction

rodeo Also called freestyle paddling. A canoe competition in which paddlers have to perform acrobatics in their boats

slalom canoe race using gates

spraydeck a cover for the cockpit, worn by the canoeist as a skirt and attached to the cockpit rim

steamer a full body wetsuit normally worn by divers. It restricts movement and is rarely used by kayakers

stern rudder a steering stroke used by surfers

stopper a dangerous re-circulating river wave, also called a hole

support stroke either a brace to provide stability during a turn or a quick slap against the water surface used to regain balance

surf ski a combination of a surf board and kayak, where the paddler sits on the board

throwline a canoeist's rescue rope, made from brightly coloured, floating material

upstream the direction the water is coming from

white water a general term for rivers of grade 2 and above. Rapids cause aeration of the water (lots of air bubbles) which makes it look white. Rapids are sometimes called wild water

x-rescue deep-water assisted rescue technique

USEFUL ADDRESSES

The British Canoe Union
Adbolton Lane
West Bridgford
Nottingham
NG2 5AS
Website: www.bcu.org.uk

Amateur Canoe Association of Western
Australia
PO Box 28
Wembly
Western Australia
6014

The International Canoe Federation
1143.Budapest
Dózsa György 't 1-3
Hungary
Website: www.datanet.hu/icf_hq/

FURTHER READING

Magazines

Canoeist, S J Fisher

Paddles, Freestyle Publications Ltd

Books

Kayak Canoeing, Know the Game, British
Canoe Union, A&C Black

Water Sports, An Outdoor Adventure
Handbook, Hugh McManners, Dorling
Kindersley

Websites

www.canoeslalom.freeserve.co.uk
(*Precision*, the newspaper of British Canoe
Slalom)

www.canoe.org.au (Australian Canoeing
online)

INDEX